fresh appetizers

Chef
express

Published by:
TRIDENT REFERENCE PUBLISHING
801 12th Avenue South, Suite 400
Naples, Fl 34102 USA

Tel: + 1 (239) 649-7077
www.tridentreference.com
email: sales@tridentreference.com

fresh
appetizers

Fresh Appetizers
© TRIDENT REFERENCE PUBLISHING

Publisher
Simon St. John Bailey

Editor-in-chief
Susan Knightley

Prepress
Precision Prep & Press

Includes Index
ISBN 1582796505
UPC 6 15269 96505 4

Printed in The United States

introduction

Perfect with drinks when getting together
with friends, for snacks while watching a
movie or on family picnics, even when
improvising a fast lunch or light supper, these
finger foods are a magic resource for cooks
on the spot. To serve and enjoy them, keep in
mind these basic guidelines.

- In all cases, the presentation and cutting of vegetables and meats for appetizers should be meticulous.
- Cheeses, spread sauces like mayonnaise, aioli (garlic mayonnaise), eggplant caviar (smashed eggplant with garlic and olive oil), tapenade (paste of olives and anchovies), pâtés, salmon and avocado are some essential ingredients.
- To accelerate the preparation to maximum speed, it's best to choose some original snow-pea boats or an all time classic like guacamole.
- Foccacias and toasts or grilled breads go well with spread pastes and can be topped with eggs in quarters, chopped olives, pan-fried slices of spring onions, or whatever your imagination may suggest.

- Pan-frying, the fast cooking technique par excellence, offers options as simple as carrot meatballs, or as sophisticated as cheese cigars with cilantro pesto.
- More complex and subtle are the potato skins with different toppings or the zucchini filled with pork, ginger and cayenne pepper.
- Those who can spare a couple of hours to marinate delights can try lamb and mango kebabs or spicy Indian-style chicken.
- Blue cheese, Parmesan, onion and sesame seed crackers are a complete option in themselves, the same as polenta cups filled with meat and beans.
- Other veggie varieties are easy eggplant and mozzarella cakes or fancy spinach and cheese mini quiches.

Difficulty scale

■□□ I Easy to do

■■□ I Requires attention

■■■ I Requires experience

snow pea boats with minted cream cheese

■ ■ □ | Cooking time: 1 minute - Preparation time: 35 minutes

ingredients
> **18 snow peas, trimmed**
> **125 g/4 oz cream cheese**
> **30 g/1 oz butter**
> **60 g/2 oz fresh mint leaves, finely chopped**
> **1 teaspoon sugar**
> **1 teaspoon horseradish relish**

method
1. Drop snow peas into a saucepan of boiling water (a) and cook for 1 minute. Drain and refresh under cold running water. Pat dry on absorbent paper.
2. Beat cream cheese and butter together until smooth. Add mint, sugar and horseradish. Slit snow peas along one edge (b) with a sharp knife or scissors. Spoon or pipe cream cheese mixture into snow peas (c). Refrigerate until firm.

....

Serves 6

tip from the chef
Snow peas are edible pea pods. To prepare for cooking, top and tail with a sharp knife and pull away strings from older, larger peas. Snow peas can be steamed, boiled, microwaved or stir-fried.

a

b

c

cherry tomatoes with parmesan

.nd rosemary

■□□ | Cooking time: 1 minute - Preparation time: 25 minutes

method

1. Sprinkle the inside of tomatoes with black pepper.
2. In a small bowl, combine cheese, cream, nutmeg and rosemary, mix well.
3. Spoon mixture into the tomatoes and grill for 1 minute. Serve immediately.

....

Serves 4

ingredients

> **1 punnet cherry tomatoes, halved and seeded**
> **black pepper**
> **1/4 cup grated Parmesan cheese**
> **1 tablespoon cream**
> **pinch nutmeg**
> **1 tablespoon fresh rosemary, finely chopped**

tip from the chef

When buying tomatoes for being stuffed, choose those that are firm and even-sized.

guacamole
with corn chips

■□□ | Cooking time: 1/2 minute - Preparation time: 25 minutes

ingredients

> **3 avocados**
> **2 small tomatoes**
> **1 small onion, very finely chopped**
> **3 red chilies, chopped**
> **2 tablespoons fresh coriander, chopped**
> **2 tablespoons lemon juice**
> **2 x 200 g/6¹/2 oz packets corn chips**

method

1. Cut avocados in half, remove stone (a) and skin (b). Mash roughly with a fork.
2. Plunge tomatoes into boiling water for 30 seconds, remove. Peel off skin, cut into quarters, remove and discard seeds. Cut tomatoes into small dice (c).
3. Combine avocado, tomato, onion, chili, coriander and lemon juice (d). Serve with corn chips for dipping.

....

Serves 8

tip from the chef

The famous Mexican specialty is also delicious served as a side dish for grilled meats.

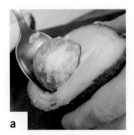

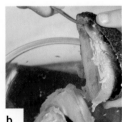

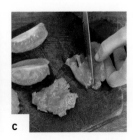

a   b   c

d

artichoke
savories

■□□ | Cooking time: 10-15 minutes - Preparation time: 25 minutes

method

1. Using a 5 cm/2 in biscuit cutter, cut out 12 circles of bread. Brush both sides of each bread circle with a little oil and place on a baking tray lined with nonstick baking paper and bake at 200°C/400°F/Gas 6 for 10-15 minutes or until bread is golden and toasted.
2. Place mayonnaise, cream, chives and black pepper to taste in a small bowl and mix to combine.
3. To assemble, top each bread circle with half an artichoke heart, a spoonful of mayonnaise mixture, a little red pepper and a sprig of dill. Serve immediately.

Makes 12

ingredients

> **12 slices bread**
> **3 tablespoons vegetable oil**
> **1/4 cup/60 g/2 oz mayonnaise**
> **1 tablespoon cream (double)**
> **1 tablespoon snipped fresh chives**
> **freshly ground black pepper**
> **2 tablespoons finely chopped red pepper**
> **440 g/14 oz canned artichoke hearts, drained and halved**
> **12 sprigs fresh dill**

tip from the chef

For these savories, the toast rounds and the mayonnaise can be made in advance, but leave the assembly until just prior to serving or the toast will go soggy.

smoked
salmon bagels

■□□ I Cooking time: 0 minutes - Preparation time: 25 minutes

ingredients

> **4 bagels, split**
> **125 g/4 oz cream cheese, softened**
> **2 tablespoons snipped fresh chives**
> **250 g/8 oz smoked salmon slices**
> **1 onion, thinly sliced**
> **1 avocado, stoned, peeled and sliced**
> **1 tablespoon capers, drained**
> **1 tablespoon lemon juice**

method

1. Spread each bagel half with cream cheese and sprinkle with chives. Top bagel halves with salmon, onion, avocado and capers. Sprinkle with lemon juice and serve immediately.

....

Serves 4

tip from the chef

A tomato and onion salad is a delicious side dish. To make salad, arrange sliced tomatoes and very thinly sliced onion on a lettuce-lined dish. Sprinkle with chopped fresh basil and drizzle with French dressing. Season to taste with black pepper.

greek
tuna focaccia

■☐☐ | Cooking time: 5 minutes - Preparation time: 20 minutes

method

1. Split focaccia bread horizontally and toast lightly under a preheated medium grill.
2. Top each piece of bread with feta cheese, rocket or watercress, tuna, sun-dried tomatoes, capers and onion rings. Sprinkle with dill.

Serves 4

ingredients

- > **2 x 10 cm/4 in squares focaccia bread**
- > **90 g/3 oz marinated or plain feta cheese, crumbled**
- > **1/2 bunch rocket or watercress, broken into sprigs**
- > **440 g/14 oz canned tuna in brine or springwater, drained**
- > **60 g/2 oz sun-dried tomatoes in oil, drained and sliced**
- > **1 tablespoon capers, drained**
- > **1 onion, thinly sliced into rings**
- > **1 tablespoon chopped fresh dill**

tip from the chef

Another variation is to make a paste with cooked fish, black olives, cream cheese and fresh coriander. Spread on toasted bread, garnish with thinly sliced spring onions.

egg
and onion spirals

■□□ | Cooking time: 0 minutes - Preparation time: 20 minutes

ingredients
> **1 loaf unsliced wholemeal bread**
> **125 g/4 oz butter, softened**

egg and spring onion filling
> **8 hard-boiled eggs**
> **4 spring onions, finely chopped**
> **2 tablespoons mayonnaise**
> **2 tablespoons sour cream**
> **2 teaspoons dry mustard**

method
1. To make filling, place eggs in a bowl and mash. Add spring onions, mayonnaise, sour cream and mustard and mix well to combine.
2. Butter the bread and spread filling over it evenly with a spatula. Roll up tightly, wrap in plastic film and chill until firm. Remove from fridge, unwrap and slice.

....
Makes 25

tip from the chef
These rolls are delicious when matched with a chilled, slightly sparkling Chardonnay wine.

classic
bruschetta

■□□ | Cooking time: 3 minutes - Preparation time: 10 minutes

method

1. Grill ciabatta slices on each side for 2-3 minutes.
2. Brush with olive oil, spread with sun-dried tomato paste, then top with bocconcini slices and shredded basil leaves, or whole leaves.

Serves 6

ingredients

> 1 ciabatta loaf, cut in 1^1/2 cm/^{1}/2 in slices
> 60 ml/2 fl oz olive oil
> ^{1}/2 cup/80 g/2^1/2 oz sun-dried tomato paste
> 180 g/6 oz bocconcini, each ball shredded into 5 slices
> ^{1}/2 cup/45 g/1^1/2 oz basil leaves, shredded, or whole leaves

tip from the chef

Ciabatta is an Italian bread made from pizza dough: 450 g/1 lb flour, 15 g/^{1}/2 oz fresh yeast, a pinch of sugar, 1 teaspoon salt and 4 tablespoons olive oil.

herb
liver pâté

■□□ | Cooking time: 12 minutes - Preparation time: 35 minutes

ingredients

> **185 g/6 oz butter,** softened
> **1 onion, chopped**
> **2 cloves garlic, chopped**
> **2 tablespoons fresh thyme** leaves
> **1 tablespoon fresh** rosemary leaves
> **750 g/1½ lb fresh** chicken livers, cleaned and trimmed, coarsely chopped
> **pinch salt**
> **freshly ground black** pepper
> **75 g/2½ oz melba** toasts or rice crackers
> **125 g/4 oz stuffed green** olives, sliced

method

1. Melt 60 g/2 oz of the butter in a frying pan over a low heat, add onion, garlic, thyme and rosemary and cook, stirring, for 6-8 minutes or until onion is very tender.
2. Add livers to pan, increase heat to medium and cook, stirring, until livers are brown on the outside, but still pink in the center. Set aside to cool.
3. Place liver mixture in a food processor, add remaining butter, salt and black pepper to taste and process until smooth. Spoon mixture into a piping bag fitted with a large star nozzle and pipe rosettes onto melba toasts or rice crackers. Arrange on a serving plate, garnish with olive slices and serve.

Makes about 30

tip from the chef
The secret of these tidbits is to present them topping crisp thin crackers or pumpernickel slices.

tuna melts

■☐☐ | Cooking time: 7 minutes - Preparation time: 25 minutes

method

1. Sauté the onion in the butter till soft and golden. Add the drained tuna, salt, pepper and Tabasco. Stir to mix ingredients and to flake the tuna. Allow to cool.

2. Place a teaspoonful of mixture on each water cracker biscuit. Cut each cheese slice into strips. Place a few strips over tuna mixture on each biscuit.

3. Cut a slice of gherkin and place on top. Set under hot grill until cheese melts and the tuna mixture is covered.

ingredients

> 1 small onion, finely chopped
> 2 teaspoons butter
> 185 g/6 1/4 oz canned tuna in oil, drained
> salt and pepper
> 1/4 teaspoon Tabasco
> 16 water cracker biscuits
> 4 sandwich cheese slices
> 2 sweet gherkins

....
Serves 4

tip from the chef

To avoid soda crackers from getting soft, prepare tidbits right before serving.

cheese cigars
with coriander pesto

■■□ | Cooking time: 10 minutes - Preparation time: 30 minutes

ingredients

- > **12 slices white sandwich bread, crusts removed**
- > **2 teaspoons prepared English mustard**
- > **4 tablespoons finely grated fresh Parmesan cheese**
- > **1/2 cup grated mozzarella cheese**
- > **1 tablespoon snipped fresh chives**
- > **cayenne pepper**
- > **1 egg, lightly beaten**
- > **vegetable oil for cooking**

coriander pesto

- > **3 large bunches fresh coriander**
- > **2 cloves garlic, crushed**
- > **60 g/2 oz pine nuts**
- > **1/2 cup/120 ml/4 fl oz olive oil**
- > **2/3 cup grated fresh Parmesan cheese**

method

1. Roll each slice of bread with a rolling pin, to flatten as much as possible.
2. Combine mustard, Parmesan cheese, mozzarella cheese, chives and cayenne pepper to taste in a bowl. Divide mixture between bread slices and spread over half of each bread slice. Brush unspread sides of bread slices with egg. Roll each slice up tightly using the egg to seal rolls. Arrange side by side on a tray. Cover and refrigerate until ready to cook.
3. Heat 2 cm/3/4 inch oil in a skillet. When hot, cook cigars a few at a time until evenly golden all over. Drain on paper towels.
4. To make pesto, place coriander leaves, garlic and pine nuts in a food processor or blender and process until finely chopped. With machine running slowly, pour in oil and process mixture until smooth. Add cheese and process to blend. Serve with hot cigars.

....
Makes 12

tip from the chef

A pesto made of coriander is the accompaniment to these tasty cheese cigars – serve as an indulgent snack or as a pre-dinner treat.

carrot balls

a

■ ■ □ | Cooking time: 5 minutes - Preparation time: 45 minutes

method

1. Place carrots, orange rind, Swiss cheese, Parmesan cheese, mint, black pepper to taste and half the egg mixture in a bowl (a) and mix to combine. Shape carrot mixture into balls.

2. Place bran and almonds in a bowl and mix to combine. Roll balls in flour, then dip in remaining egg mixture and roll in bran mixture (b). Place balls on a plate lined with plastic food wrap and refrigerate for 30 minutes.

3. Heat oil in a large saucepan until a cube of bread dropped in browns in 50 seconds (c). Cook balls, a few at a time, for 4-5 minutes or until golden (d) and heated through. Drain on absorbent kitchen paper and serve immediately.

....
Serves 4

ingredients

> **3 carrots, grated**
> **2 teaspoons orange rind**
> **60 g/2 oz grated Swiss cheese**
> **60 g/2 oz grated Parmesan cheese**
> **1 tablespoon chopped fresh mint**
> **freshly ground black pepper**
> **2 eggs, lightly beaten**
> **1 cup/30 g/1 oz unprocessed bran**
> **3 tablespoons finely chopped almonds**
> **flour**
> **vegetable oil for deep-frying**

tip from the chef

These carrot balls make for great starters when served with a green salad.

b

c

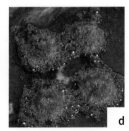
d

cheese puffs

■■□ | Cooking time: 5 minutes - Preparation time: 30 minutes

ingredients

> **4 cups/500 g/1 lb grated tasty cheese**
> **1 cup/90 g/3 oz fresh breadcrumbs**
> **4 eggs, separated**
> **1 teaspoon dry mustard**
> **1 teaspoon paprika**
> **salt and pepper**
> **fresh breadcrumbs, extra**
> **oil for deep frying**

method

1. Combine cheese, breadcrumbs, egg yolks, mustard, paprika, salt and pepper (a). Mix well.
2. Beat egg whites until stiff. Gently fold into the cheese mixture (b).
3. Shape mixture into small, walnut sized, balls. Roll in extra breadcrumbs (c).
4. Deep fry, a few at a time (d), until golden brown, about 30 seconds.

....
Serves 4

tip from the chef
Serve them real hot, using small skewers.

a

b

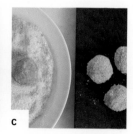
c

d

potato
croquettes

a

■ ■ □ | Cooking time: 40 minutes - Preparation time: 30 minutes

method

1. Place potatoes in a saucepan of water and bring to the boil. Reduce heat, cover and simmer for 20-25 minutes or until potatoes are cooked. Drain potatoes and press through a sieve into a bowl.

2. Add breadcrumbs, spring onions, cottage cheese, egg, parsley, oregano and black pepper to taste to potatoes (a) and mix to combine. Cover and refrigerate until potato mixture is cold.

3. Divide potato mixture into 12 portions and shape into croquettes. Roll each croquette in flour (b) and place on a plate lined with plastic food wrap.

4. Heat oil in a large saucepan until a cube of bread dropped in browns in 50 seconds. Cook a few croquettes at a time for 4-5 minutes (c) or until golden and heated through. Drain on absorbent kitchen paper and serve immediately.

Serves 4

ingredients

> **500 g/1 lb potatoes, cut into quarters**
> **100 g/3¹/₂ oz wholemeal breadcrumbs**
> **4 spring onions, chopped**
> **250 g/8 oz cottage cheese**
> **1 egg, lightly beaten**
> **1 tablespoon chopped fresh parsley**
> **1 tablespoon chopped fresh oregano or 1 teaspoon dried oregano**
> **freshly ground black pepper**
> **1¹/₂ cups/230 g/7¹/₂ oz wholemeal flour**
> **vegetable oil for deep-frying**

tip from the chef

Potato croquettes make an interesting alternative to plain potatoes when served as an accompaniment. They are also a delicious light meal, served with salad and mango chutney.

b

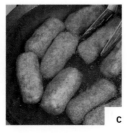

c

baby squash with pepper and cheese filling

■■□ I Cooking time: 20 minutes - Preparation time: 40 minutes

ingredients

> **24 yellow baby squash**
> **1 large red pepper, finely chopped**
> **1/2 cup/60 g/2 oz tasty cheese (mature Cheddar), grated**
> **1 egg, lightly beaten**
> **2 spring onions, finely chopped**
> **1/4 teaspoon cayenne pepper**

method

1. Cook squash in boiling water until tender, drain, cool. Scoop out top part of each squash.
2. Combine red pepper, cheese, egg, spring onions and cayenne pepper. Spoon into squash.
3. Bake at 180°C/350°F/Gas 4 for 10 minutes or until heated through.

....

Makes 24

tip from the chef

These nice baby squash can also be stuffed with a three cheese mix (blue, cream and cottage), ham and chopped onions. Then, gratin in oven.

ginger
pork zucchini

◼◼▢ | Cooking time: 25 minutes - Preparation time: 45 minutes

method

1. Wash the zucchini and cut them into 8 cm/3 in pieces. With a small sharp knife hollow out the center by removing all the seeds, being careful not to pierce the skin.
2. Put the zucchini pieces in a pot of boiling water and cook them on high heat for 3 minutes. Drain them, run them under cold water and set them aside.
3. In a large frying pan melt the butter and sauté the onion and garlic until golden in color. Do not brown them. Add the meat and cook the mixture over high heat for about 10 minutes or until the meat is completely cooked.
4. Drain on paper towels. Put the meat mixture in a food processor and add all other ingredients. Process until mixture is finely ground.
5. Carefully stuff the zucchini with the filling until firmly packed. Refrigerate them until ready to use. At serving time heat the stuffed pieces for 5-8 minutes in oven, preheated at 180°C/350°F/Gas 4. Slice them and serve immediately.

ingredients

> 6 medium zucchini

gingered pork filling

> 1 tablespoon butter
> 2 medium onions, chopped
> 2 cloves garlic, chopped
> 350 g/12 oz minced pork
> $1/2$ teaspoon ground ginger
> $1/2$ teaspoon cayenne pepper
> 1 tablespoon tomato paste
> 1 tablespoon dry white wine
> $1/8$ teaspoon salt
> dash pepper

....
Makes 36 slices

tip from the chef

Ginger and pork meat make a good match. Both strong and temperamental, they balance each other.

cheese
and chive cookies

■■□ I Cooking time: 10 minutes - Preparation time: 45 minutes

ingredients
> **1 cup/125 g/4 oz self-raising flour, sifted**
> **125 g/4 oz butter, cut into pieces**
> **60 g/2 oz hard blue cheese, crumbled**
> **2 tablespoons grated Parmesan cheese**
> **3 tablespoons snipped fresh chives**
> **4 tablespoons sesame seeds**

method
1. Place flour, butter, blue and Parmesan cheeses and chives in a food processor and process until ingredients cling together. Turn onto a lightly floured surface and knead lightly. Shape dough into a ball, wrap in plastic food wrap and chill for 30 minutes.
2. Roll heaped teaspoons of mixture into balls, then roll in sesame seeds to coat. Place balls on lightly greased baking trays, flatten slightly with a fork and bake at 220°C/425°F/Gas 7 for 10 minutes or until golden. Stand on trays for 3 minutes, then transfer to wire racks to cool. Store cookies in an airtight container.

....
Makes 30

tip from the chef
These nutritious crackers should always be served at the beginning of a meal or to complement lighter preparations and vegetables.

chili
bean corn cups

a

■ ■ ■ | Cooking time: 90 minutes - Preparation time: 45 minutes

method

1. To make pastry, place butter and cream cheese in a small bowl (a) and mix to combine. Make a ring with flour, polenta and salt; pour the previous mixture into the center and blend together to form a soft dough. Turn dough onto a lightly floured surface (b) and knead until smooth. Divide dough into small balls, press into lightly greased muffin tins (c) and bake at 180°C/350°F/Gas 4 for 20 minutes or until golden.

2. Heat oil in a frying pan over a medium heat, add onion and garlic and cook, stirring, for 5 minutes or until onion is tender. Add beef, cumin and chili powder and stir-fry for 4-5 minutes or until beef is brown.

3. Stir in tomatoes and beans and bring to the boil. Reduce heat and simmer, stirring occasionally, for 1 hour or until most of the liquid evaporates and mixture is quite dry. Season to taste with black pepper and spoon into hot polenta cups. Serve immediately.

ingredients

> **2 tablespoons vegetable oil**
> **1 large onion, chopped**
> **2 cloves garlic, crushed**
> **250 g/8 oz lean beef mince**
> **2 teaspoons ground cumin**
> **2 teaspoons chili powder**
> **440 g/14 oz canned peeled tomatoes, undrained and mashed**
> **440 g/14 oz canned red kidney beans, drained and rinsed**
> **freshly ground black pepper**

polenta pastry

> **185 g/6 oz butter**
> **185 g/6 oz cream cheese**
> **2 cups/250 g/8 oz flour**
> **1 cup/170 g/5 1/2 oz polenta**
> **pinch salt**

Makes 24

tip from the chef

Other options for filling: pan-fried ground meat with onions and thyme, mashed eggplant with garlic and olive oil, goat cheese with chopped tomatoes.

b

c

curried
sausage puffs

■ ■ □ | Cooking time: 18 minutes - Preparation time: 35 minutes

ingredients
> **2 sheets ready-rolled puff pastry**
> **375 g/³/₄ lb sausage mince**
> **1 small carrot, finely grated**
> **2 spring onions, chopped**
> **1 tablespoon fruit chutney**
> **1 teaspoon curry powder**
> **salt and pepper**

method
1. Cut pastry sheets in half.
2. Combine mince, carrot, spring onions, chutney and curry powder (a), season to taste with salt and pepper, divide into 4, roll each into a sausage shape (b) the length of the long side of the pastry.
3. Place sausage along pastry, roll up, and seal edge with water. Cut roll into 1 cm/¹/₂ in slices (c).
4. Place slices onto greased baking tray; bake at 200°C/400°F/Gas 6 for 15 minutes or until golden brown and puffed.

....
Makes 24

tip from the chef
This filling can be used to make baby phyllo pastry parcels.

a

b

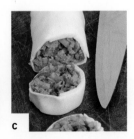

c

potato skins

■■□ | Cooking time: 40 minutes - Preparation time: 50 minutes

method

1. Preheat the oven at 180°C/350°F/Gas 4. Wash and dry each potato. Pierce with a fork and place in the preheated oven. Bake for 30 minutes or until the center is firm but can be easily pierced with a fork.
2. Cool the potato, cut in quarters lengthwise and cut out the center leaving the skin with 0.5 cm/¹/₄ in to 110 mm/¹/₂ in of potato on it.
3. Brush the skins with butter, then sprinkle them with salt and pepper. Bake for 10 minutes. Top them with chosen topping and bake for another 5-10 minutes until warmed.

Makes 4 pieces per potato

ingredients

> **baking potatoes**

bacon and mushroom topping

> potato pulp
> sautéed bacon and mushroom
> parsley

shrimp and chives topping

> potato pulp
> sour cream
> chopped fresh chives
> shrimps
> salt and pepper to taste

chicken and almond topping

> potato pulp
> cooked chicken
> toasted pine nuts
> chopped shallots
> sour cream
> black pepper

tip from the chef

Topping preparations are also good for filling pastry cases made with 175 g/6 oz flour, a pinch of salt, 90 g/3 oz refrigerated butter, 1 egg yolk and 1 tablespoon water.

mini spinach and cheese quiches

■■□ I Cooking time: 20 minutes - Preparation time: 35 minutes

ingredients
> **3 sheets ready-rolled puff pastry**
> **125 g/4 1/2 oz tasty cheese (mature Cheddar), cubed**
> **2 spinach leaves, washed and torn into large strips, with stems removed**
> **1/2 small onion, peeled and halved**
> **1 egg**
> **3 tablespoons cream**
> **1 tablespoon parsley sprigs, firmly packed**
> **1 tablespoon French mustard**
> **salt, pepper**

method
1. Cut pastry into 6 cm/2 1/2 in rounds with a pastry cutter and press into shallow patty pans.
2. In a food processor, process the cheese, spinach, onion, egg, cream, parsley, mustard, salt and pepper until all ingredients are finely chopped and well combined.
3. Spoon 1 tablespoon of mixture into each patty pan.
4. Bake at 200°C/400°F/Gas 6 for 20 minutes, or until puffed and golden.
5. Remove from pans, place on platter and serve.

....
Makes about 24

tip from the chef
Variations
- Crab and ham: Substitute for cheese, spinach and parsley with 170 g/6 oz canned crab meat, drained, and 125 g/4 1/2 oz sliced ham.
- Cheese and ham: Substitute for spinach leaves with 125 g/4 1/2 oz sliced ham.

eggplant with mozzarella cheese

■☐☐ | Cooking time: 9 minutes - Preparation time: 10 minutes

method

1. Lightly brush eggplant slices with combined oil, garlic and pepper. Grill until lightly browned, approximately 3 minutes each side.
2. Top each slice with mozzarella cheese and decorate with pimento strips.
3. Return to the grill and cook until cheese has melted. Serve immediately and garnish with fresh basil if desired.

Makes 8

ingredients

> 1 medium eggplant, cut into 1 cm/^{1}/$_2$ in slices
> 3 tablespoons olive oil
> 1 clove garlic, crushed
> ^{1}/$_4$ teaspoon pepper
> 8 thin slices mozzarella cheese
> 2 pimentos, sliced into strips
> fresh basil (optional)

tip from the chef

With eggplant you can make a dressing that goes with everything: the so-called caviar. To prepare, roast eggplants in halves till soft and pearled; peel and process with garlic, salt, pepper, paprika and lemon juice; add olive oil and keep blending to an unctuous cream.

lamb
and mango skewers

■□□ | Cooking time: 10 minutes - Preparation time: 30 minutes

ingredients

> 1 kg/2 lb lean lamb, trimmed of visible fat and cut into 2 cm/3/4 in cubes
> 3 mangoes, cut into 2 cm/3/4 in cubes

hoisin-soy marinade

> 1 tablespoon finely grated fresh ginger
> 3/4 cup/185 ml/6 fl oz hoisin sauce
> 1/4 cup/60 ml/2 fl oz reduced-salt soy sauce
> 1/4 cup/60 ml/2 fl oz rice wine vinegar
> 1/4 cup/60 ml/2 fl oz vegetable oil

method

1. Use 24 wooden skewers (a). Soak in cold water for at least 30 minutes before threading meat.
2. To make marinade, place ginger, hoisin and soy sauces, vinegar and oil in a bowl and mix to combine. Add lamb, toss to coat (b), cover and marinate in the refrigerator for at least 4 hours.
3. Thread lamb and mango cubes, alternately, onto oiled skewers (c). Cook on a preheated hot barbecue for 3-4 minutes each side or until tender.

....
Serves 8

tip from the chef

*These tasty skewers can be made with
pineapple instead of mango.*

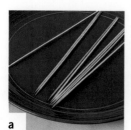

a

b

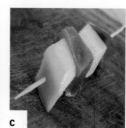

c

two-toppings
crostini

◼◻◻ | Cooking time: 12 minutes - Preparation time: 20 minutes

method

1. Brush bread slices with oil, place under a preheated hot grill and toast both sides until golden. Rub one side of toasts with cut side of garlic cloves.

2. For tomato and basil topping, top half the toast slices with some tomato, onion and basil, and grill for 1-2 minutes or until topping is warm.

3. For eggplant and feta topping, brush eggplant slices with oil and cook under preheated hot grill for 3-4 minutes each side or until lightly browned. Top remaining toasts with eggplant slices and sprinkle with feta cheese and black pepper to taste. Cook under a preheated hot grill for 1-2 minutes or until topping is warm.

....

Makes 16-20

ingredients

> **1 French bread stick, cut into 1 cm/¹/₂ in slices**
> **2 tablespoons olive oil**
> **2 cloves garlic, halved**

tomato and basil topping

> **2 tomatoes, sliced**
> **1 red onion, sliced**
> **2 tablespoons shredded basil leaves**

eggplant and feta topping

> **2 baby eggplant, sliced**
> **1 tablespoon olive oil**
> **125 g/4 oz feta cheese, crumbled**
> **freshly ground black pepper**

tip from the chef

Crostini, made from hot baguette slice toasts, can be topped with various pastes of cheese, olives or feta cheese with olive oil.

spicy indian chicken

■ ■ □ | Cooking time: 5 minutes - Preparation time: 35 minutes

ingredients

> **8 boneless chicken breast fillets, cut into 2.5 cm/1 in cubes**
> **1 cup/200 g/6 1/2 oz natural yogurt**
> **1 clove garlic, crushed**
> **1 teaspoon grated fresh ginger**
> **1/2 teaspoon garam masala**
> **1/4 teaspoon turmeric**
> **1/4 teaspoon ground cumin**
> **1 tablespoon chopped fresh coriander**
> **freshly ground black pepper**

cucumber coriander dip

> **1/2 cucumber, grated and drained**
> **1 tablespoon chopped fresh coriander**
> **1/2 cup/100 g/3 1/2 oz natural yogurt**
> **1/4 cup/60 ml/2 fl oz cream (double)**
> **freshly ground black pepper**

method

1. Place chicken, yogurt, garlic, ginger, garam masala, turmeric, cumin, coriander and black pepper to taste in a bowl and toss to combine. Cover and refrigerate for at least 4 hours or overnight.

2. Remove chicken from yogurt mixture and place in a single layer on a lightly greased baking tray. Cook under a preheated grill, for 5 minutes or until cooked. Spear 1 or 2 pieces of chicken onto wooden toothpicks.

3. To make dip, squeeze excess liquid from cucumber. Place cucumber, coriander, yogurt, cream and black pepper to taste in a bowl and mix to combine. Serve with chicken for dipping.

....
Serves 8

tip from the chef

Instead of cutting the chicken fillets into pieces, you can marinate them whole, then grill and serve with rice and salad for a tasty meal.

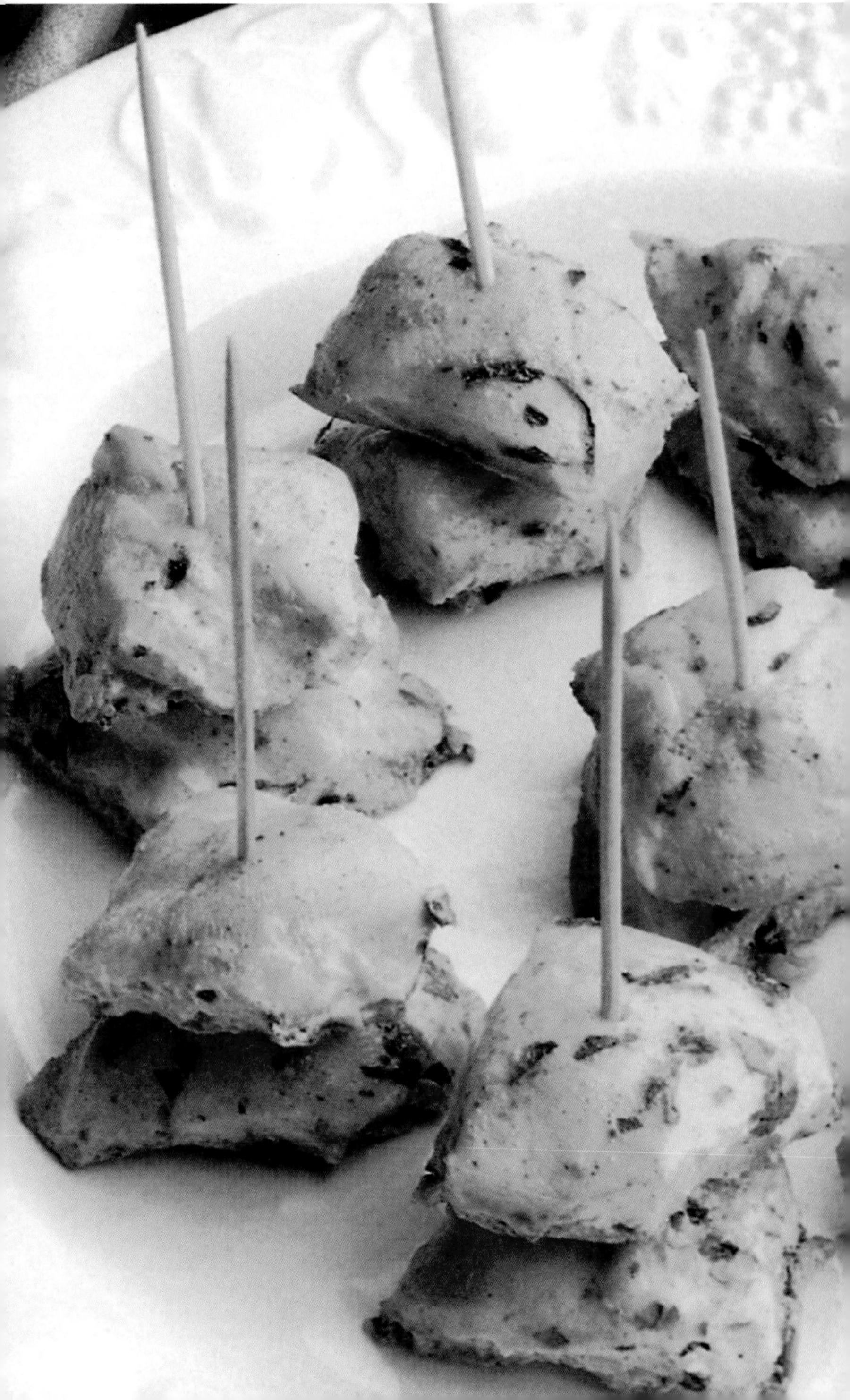

antipasto
skewers

■■□ | Cooking time: 5 minutes - Preparation time: 30 minutes

method

1. Place rosemary leaves, thyme leaves, vinegar and oil in a bowl and whisk to combine. Cut eggplant and zucchini into cubes. Add to vinegar mixture, then add tomatoes and red pepper. Toss to coat vegetables with marinade, cover and marinate for 30-60 minutes.

2. To make dipping sauce, place pesto, sour cream and black pepper to taste in a bowl and mix to combine.

3. Preheat barbecue to a high heat. Roll salami slices tightly. Drain vegetables and reserve marinade. Thread vegetables and salami rolls, alternately, onto small skewers. Cook skewers, brushing frequently with reserved marinade, on oiled barbecue grill for 1-2 minutes each side or until vegetables are tender. Serve skewers warm with dipping sauce.

Makes 12

ingredients

> 1 tablespoon fresh rosemary leaves
> 1 tablespoon fresh thyme leaves
> 1/4 cup/60 ml/2 fl oz balsamic vinegar
> 2 tablespoons olive oil
> 2 baby eggplant, halved lengthwise
> 2 zucchini, halved lengthwise
> 155 g/5 oz semi-dried tomatoes
> 1 red pepper, diced
> 250 g/8 oz sliced spicy salami

creamy pesto dipping sauce

> 1/4 cup/60 ml/2 fl oz pesto
> 1/2 cup/125 g/4 oz sour cream
> freshly ground black pepper

tip from the chef

These skewers are best enjoyed before barbecues or outdoor lunches.

thai barbecue
fish cakes

■□□ I Cooking time: 3 minutes - Preparation time: 20 minutes

ingredients
> **375 g/12 oz boneless, fine fleshed, white fish fillets, chopped**
> **2 tablespoons red curry paste**
> **1 stalk fresh lemon grass, chopped or 1/2 teaspoon dried lemon grass, soaked in hot water until soft**
> **1 tablespoon chopped fresh coriander**
> **4 kaffir lime leaves, finely shredded**
> **1 egg white**
> **lime wedges**
> **sweet chili sauce**

method
1. Place fish, curry paste, lemon grass, coriander, lime leaves and egg white in a food processor and process until smooth.
2. Using wet or lightly oiled hands, take 1 tablespoon of mixture and roll into a ball, then flatten to form a disk. Repeat with remaining mixture. Place fish cakes on a tray lined with plastic food wrap and chill for 30 minutes or until firm.
3. Preheat barbecue to a high heat. Place fish cakes on oiled barbecue plate and cook for 1 minute each side or until cooked through. Serve with lime wedges and sweet chili sauce.

....
Makes 18

tip from the chef
These fish burgers go well with a fresh salad of bean sprouts, grated carrots and shredded cabbage.

tomato
salsa on bruschetta

■☐☐ | Cooking time: 8 minutes - Preparation time: 25 minutes

method

1. Preheat barbecue to a medium heat. To make the dressing, place garlic cloves on barbecue plate and cook for 1-2 minutes each side or until flesh is soft. Squeeze flesh from garlic cloves and mash. Place garlic, vinegar and oil in a screwtop jar and shake to combine.

2. To make salsa, place tomatoes and 2 tablespoons oil in a bowl and toss to coat. Place tomatoes, cut side down, on barbecue plate and cook for 1 minute each side. Place tomatoes, cheese, basil and black peppercorns to taste in a bowl, add dressing and toss to combine.

3. Lightly brush bread with oil, place on barbecue grill and toast for 1 minute each side. To serve, pile tomato salsa onto bread and serve immediately.

ingredients

> **12 slices crusty Italian bread**

grilled tomato salsa

> **500 g/1 lb cherry tomatoes, halved**
> **olive oil**
> **6 small bocconcini cheeses, chopped**
> **4 tablespoons torn fresh basil leaves**
> **crushed black peppercorns**

roasted garlic dressing

> **2 cloves garlic, unpeeled**
> **2 tablespoons balsamic vinegar**
> **1 tablespoon olive oil**

....
Makes 12

tip from the chef

Tomato, mozzarella and basil, with some drops of olive oil and a few turns of the pepper grinder, make up a unique and irreplaceable combination. As a salad, topping pizza crust, hot or cold, always delicious and welcome.

mediterranean
skewers

■■■ | Cooking time: 40 minutes - Preparation time: 1 hour

method

1. Place oregano and oil in a bowl. Add eggplant, zucchini, onions and peppers, toss to coat. Cover and stand 30-60 minutes.
2. To make focaccia, dissolve yeast with 1/2 cup lukewarm water and sugar. Combine flour and salt, place in a food processor and add yeast mixture. Process while gradually adding lukewarm water to form a dough. Cover with plastic food wrap and stand in a warm place until dough rises lightly. Roll out dough on a floured surface and place on an oiled baking tray. Sprinkle with grated cheese, coarse salt and oregano. Bake at 220°C/440°F/Gas 7 until golden and crisp. Cut diagonally into bars.
3. Preheat barbecue at high heat. Drain vegetables and reserve marinade. Thread vegetables and cheese, alternately, in skewers. Cook on grill, brushing frequently with marinade, 1-2 minutes each side or until vegetables are tender. Serve skewers with focaccia bars and garnish with fresh oregano.

Serves 8

ingredients

> 1 tablespoon chopped fresh oregano
> 8 tablespoons olive oil
> 2 eggplant, cut into thick slices
> 2 zucchini, cut into thick slices
> 2 onions, quartered
> 1 red pepper, cubed
> 1 green pepper, cubed
> 250 g/8 oz fontina cheese, cubed

oregano focaccia

> 15 g/1/2 oz fresh yeast
> 1 teaspoon sugar
> 250 g/8 oz flour
> 1 teaspoon salt
> 3 tablespoons olive oil
> 60 g/2 oz Parmesan cheese, grated
> 1 tablespoon coarse salt
> 1 tablespoon chopped fresh oregano
> fresh oregano to garnish

tip from the chef

These Mediterranean skewers can also be made with other vegetables, such as fennel, celery, cardoon. To vary and enhance aroma of focaccia, use chopped rosemary and garlic instead of oregano.

index